Another Slice of Chocolate Cake

Another Slice of
Chocolate Cake

Poems for Those Who Grieve

Shirley Biggerstaff Wright

FOREWORD BY
George H. Grant

RESOURCE *Publications* · Eugene, Oregon

ANOTHER SLICE OF CHOCOLATE CAKE
Poems for Those Who Grieve

Resource Publications
An Imprint of Wipf and Stock Publishers
199 W. 8th Ave., Suite 3
Eugene, OR 97401

www.wipfandstock.com

PAPERBACK ISBN: 979-8-3852-0624-7
HARDCOVER ISBN: 979-8-3852-0625-4
EBOOK ISBN: 979-8-3852-0626-1

VERSION NUMBER 01/03/24

Dedicated to

My beloved family, especially my husband Ken,
who shore me up when times are tough.

Whole Family Medicine, Decatur Georgia.

Winship Cancer Center of Emory University, Atlanta, Georgia.

Persons around the world struggling
with metastatic breast cancer.

Contents

Foreword

Be forewarned, this tender account is uncomfortable to read. There is good reason for that. At once, a reader is challenged to go on a deeply personal and raw journey of the heart that wrenches the soul of anyone who has one. Unfolding is the story of a faithful and faithfilled participant/observer who weaves songs of lament with journalistic witness to death and not death. With the brush of a poet our storyteller demands that we honor and respect what it feels like to face the limits of living and the utter depravity of losing. Please take your time and sit with each piece over days and weeks or longer. To digest it all quickly will require an obscenely large placemat because valued bites will not be contained on your plate, and you may find yourself emotionally overwhelmed from the sitting. Like our artist, I, too, sit in my own darkness and witness the sweetness of sorrows in the careseekers to whom I am beholden. I only aspire to the courage it takes to tell the God's Honest Truth of what it means to be at once blessed and cursed with a mind of knowing bliss and accepting that I cannot hang on to it. I attest through my knowing Shirley Wright 38 years ago and still today, that she is that courageous lyricist and musician to those who are in pain. If you feign wellness, you will not hear her music. Take your time. Hum along in your own way. Get in your reps. After all, we are all going to the "end of the line".

—George H. Grant, MDiv, PhD
  Spiritual Health
  Woodruff Health Sciences Center
  Emory University

Introduction

Readers may think about favorite chapters of books they are reading, chapters so wonderful that it is sad approaching their ending. The converse is also true. Details of some chapters are so painful the reader simply wants to slam the covers shut never to open them again. So it is with our lives—points so wonderful that we would wish they would go on forever, other ones so painful we are left to ask as does the Psalmist, "How long, O Lord, how long?"

A metastatic breast cancer diagnosis some three years ago was just such a chapter in my life. Most grief-filled chapters of our lives prompt responses such as closing eyes and wishing they would all go away or pledging the best of coping mechanisms if only there can be a guarantee that it will be over soon. Unfortunately, grief experiences are never something that will go away as we lie down and close our eyes, nor will we be able to make quick end of them. In the case of metastatic disease, we cannot see an end at all until we close our eyes in death.

So what helps? Being honest about our feelings is imperative. Finding ways to express those feelings is critical; however, finding places to do so can sometimes prove illusive. In 2021 I began writing grief poetry to reflect on the confounding feelings associated with a terminal illness. One poem turned into another and into another. That process pressed me into reflection on grief situations through my ministry in the United Methodist Church, all of which ultimately became *Chocolate Cake and Other Losses: Poems about Grief.*

The grief process nor the writing did not end there. Over the last year, continued reflection on my personal situation as well as sad stories I encountered in ministry provide the basis for *Another Slice of Chocolate Cake: Poems for Those Who Grieve.* I see these poems as reflecting movement along a continuum of grief. Initially overwhelmed, almost paralyzed, I felt unable even to pray. Since the lament Psalms have been significant in my academic life, I found myself returning to them as part of my coping with disease. My poems do not follow the exact pattern of the Psalms of Lament; however, they bring my honest struggle before God. While a sense of unfairness about my situation pervades many of the poems in the first book, *Another Slice of Chocolate Cake: Poems for Those Who Grieve* concludes with a poem entitled, "Thanks for the Ride." This and other poems in the volume show something of a sense of humor now present in my day-to-day handling of grief, but more importantly, I can now look on my life, see the good years that I have had, testify to God's presence through them all, and I can say thank you or "Thanks for the ride!" It is a God-given one.

As you find yourself shrouded in grief, I encourage you to write. The words do not even have to be intended for anyone else to read. As we confine words to paper, they somehow lighten our loads and help us to persevere, even to live with a sense of gratitude for all that God has given in a good and positive way.

Another Slice of Chocolate Cake

We played up
in fine style,
the fact that he,
the birthday boy,
would get the first
slice of chocolate cake,
one with the
letter "M" on top.

All too eagerly
he grasped the plate,
the slice of chocolate
cake tumbling to the
floor, and there was
no consoling him.

Quickly we sliced
another piece of
chocolate cake, but
his response was a
"No! It's not the
first one—one with
the 'M' on top."

And so it is with us,
never a replacement person,
or home, or child; instead,
we simply remember
and somehow move on.

Grief Is . . .

Mate dies of cancer, age sixty-eight,
Job lost to downsizing, age fifty-five,
Children leave home, age forty-seven,
Long-distance move away from family, age thirty-four,
Leaving school, age twenty-two,
Grandparent dies, age eighteen.

An exhaustive list?
Utterly impossible,
For grief is
The sum total
Of all our
Losses.

Lies

We hate all of them,
But the worst are the ones
We tell ourselves.

"He was a jerk,
Better off without him."

"House up in smoke,
Old and dilapidated anyway!"

"Cancer changed me?
No, lived with gratitude anyway!"

Hard to admit the truth,
But, oh, so important!

Until we've admitted the loss,
Until we've grieved,
We can't move on!

And I never knew gratitude
For every single day,
Until I saw life
Hanging in the balance!

Choices

Big ones,
Small ones,
Important,
Not-so-important.

Foods to eat,
Places to go,
Schools to attend.
Jobs to pursue,
A life-long mate,
Then one . . .

A category
All of its own.

How to die,
Side effects
Of drugs?
The disease
Itself?

Anger

Anger . . .

We have it,
Plenty of it.

Not just the garden variety,
Not like the first time around.

Rest assured, with recurrence it's
A seething, all-consuming rage.

Can anyone blame us?
Isn't once enough?

Diabolical treatments to undergo
All for the promise of bright futures.

Clanging bells that announce closure
To our dark chapters.

But all too soon a new chapter unfolds
Darker than the one before.

What now? What shall we do with our . . .
Anger?

Pro-Life

I'm pro-life!

Oh, it's not what
You might think.

It's about me . . .
    About my decision
        To keep on choosing . . .

Life,

Despite the horrible
    Side effect of drugs,
        Fatigue, nausea, days when
            I feel that I'm already . . .

Dead.

We Wait

Same old,
Same old.

Heightened worry,
Anticipation of
News from
Scans, Good?
Bad? How
Can one
Prepare for
Both the
Same time?

Somehow we
Manage, we
Put on
Brave faces,
March into
Contraptions that
Read our
Bodies like
A map,
And then,
We wait.

Be It Resolved

Be it hereby resolved . . .

I give up grumbling,
Complaining, and most of all,
Feeling sorry for myself.

After all, I've had
A good life, should
It end tomorrow,
I can count
My blessings—loving family,
Warm home, and
Seventy-one years to date.

So I banish complaints
Of aching bones,
Side effects of drugs,
And worry about
The future.

Be it resolved: I will live for today
And be grateful.

Now, O Lord, empower my resolve!

To the Bitter End

I can't tell . . .

Do I really hear your voice,
or is it my imagination
playing tricks on me?

Those on the outside
always criticize us,
laugh and say it's all a great big hoax.

I've never had
so much trouble before,
but isn't that always true?

Good times come,
we bow and say "Thank you,"
but altogether different as times are bad.

And when it's very,
bad—those times especially
we wonder, "Are they true . . .

These stories of faith and can I
really hear your voice
whispering reassurance, saying you'll be with me?"

I choose to believe,
choose to trust the words
hanging in the wind, rustling in my ear . . .

"I'll be with you to the bitter end."

Even Now

Whoever said that life is easy?
Certainly, not I,
For I am an island, and
Daily the waves beat upon my shore.

Tenaciously I endure their violence,
Sometimes close to despair,
But then I find strength in some unexpected
Visitor to my shore, calling me to hope again.

And I do hope, and I rest
In my renewed awareness,
Of the years of battering that have beset my shores
While still I endured.

And I will *survive* . . .
Even now!

It's Okay

It's okay
to rant,
okay to
make a
long list
of grievances,
then to
conclude with,
"It's unfair."

It's okay
because we
stand in
a long
line of
ranters, complainers,
ones who've
shouted their
perceived unfairness.

For we,
too, will
ultimately return
to our
our faith
in God
with us
through thick
and thin.

Un-grieved

I just figured it out,
It's taken me two whole years,
I've been doing all sorts of stuff,
And I've figured it out.

Ever since the doctor said the word,
"Terminal," I've been thinking,
Processing best as I could,
The things that need to be done,

The thoughts that need to be thought,
My study from long ago told me,
There's a name for these endeavors,
Scholars call it life review.

But for days and days on end,
I've found myself recalling,
Some happy, yes, but mostly
The stuff of a different sort.

This time I'm not going to brush
It all away nor command tears
Remain in their lacrimal space,
For in the midst of grieving an unwanted diagnosis . . .

I must also
Grieve the, as yet, un-grieved.

Leaving You

I never thought
It could happen,
Leaving you the furthest
Thing from my mind.

Always thought it'd be
You who'd leave me, and
I've practiced it over and over
Again, how I'd cope.

Leave the memory-filled house?
Move near a kid?
Take up a new hobby?
Reinvent myself?

The statistics went haywire—
At least in our case,
But I'm learning it's just as hard
To think of leaving you . . .

As it was to think of
Your leaving me,
After all, who is each of us
Apart from one another?

Been There—Comb My Hair

Been there,
Saw the adoring looks,
The sweet conversation around her
As news first leaked
About her demise.

Been there,
Saw the climate change,
How they closed the door,
Went in to check on her
Less and less.

Been there,
Showed me into her room,
She a shell of her former self,
And they talk of her as though
She's not there.

Been there,
Saw how pitiful she looked,
Once the glamour queen,
But now she lies in bed,
Hair standing every direction.

Been there,
Witness to their growing distance,
Pulling away more each day,
As though the distance might
Salve their pain.

I'm here,
Same place as she,
So I'm begging, "Stay with me,
Talk to me and, please,
Comb my hair."

Coping Mechanisms

Life is never easy,
So much loss,
So many fears.

She died,
Only forty-nine years
On this earth.

Losing her left
A hole in my heart
Too big to mend.

Over time,
Along with the grief came fear
Like I had never known.

Her genes—did they
Spell doom for me—early death
A foregone conclusion?

I summoned from deep
Within me my
Very best coping skills.

Thoughts of Granddaddy,
Her dad, who lived
Well into his nineties.

It brightened my days,
Sustained me, this remembrance
Of Granddaddy's longevity genes.

The diagnosis—it shakes me
To the very core, but still
Others have beaten it.

So I held on,
Kept the image of Granddaddy
Firmly in my head.

But now—now what?
The new diagnosis—stage four—
The picture of Granddaddy is fading.

Puzzle

The box is open,
It lies in front of us.

The work begins, a daunting task,
the hardest ever undertaken.

Sort, arrange in ways that make sense,
Try first one fit, then another.

Push ahead, persevere,
The task seems manageable, less daunting.

Someone comes along,
Tips the table, pieces in disarray.

And so it is with the diagnosis, treatable not curable,
But against odds, finding ways to cope.

Then comes something new—a cough, a new pain—
And everything—all the painstaking work—is in disarray.

Shifting Gears

The old truck sat in the driveway,
And like any country girl
I was supposed to master
The shifts from first to second
To third without stalling out.

Driving in the fields
Far from any worries
About a false start with the clutch,
I overcame any thoughts
About rolling backwards into another car . . .

I did my duty and to others
I even looked competent,
But here, all grown up,
Body plagued with disease,
Yet, held at bay by wonder drugs, how do I
Shift gears from imminent death to life once again?

Trust

Trust . . .

It's hard to come by,
And when it's gone,
It's gone.

We had placed it with them,
There was really nothing else we
Could do.

Slowly, bit by bit,
They took their toll until she
Was gone.

Now they're asking
Me to grant it them
Still again.

What a thing to ask—trust drugs,
Ones whose side effects often kill same as the
Disease itself!

When it's gone it's gone—well, maybe not,
Least not when it seems there are no
Other options.

It's What We Do

It's what we do!

Grieved her loss,
Prayed the prayers,
Asked the questions,
Would it happen—
Happen to me?

No! Certainly not,
Far too cruel,
Would never experience
Her same fate,
Perhaps heart attack
Late in life,
Accident while riding
Fun mountain road,
Thought I'd heard
"Never, no never,
Happen to you."

Did due diligence,
The yearly tests,
The pink envelope
Delivered by mail.
Then one day
Got bad news.
Scheduled more tests,

Got the result,
Yes, it'd happened,
As to her!

Had the surgery
All the rest,
Prayed still harder,
"Help me overcome,
Let it be
One and done!"

Thought I'd heard,
"Yes, that's it,
One and done!'
Tuck it away,
Decided I'd be
Like Granddaddy, longevity
Genes I'd received.

Kept me going,
Free from worry,
Until one day
Denial stopped working,
'Cause word came,
"You're stage four!"
Still I'm glad,
Propped me up,
Kept me going.

Denial—
It's what we do!

There with You

When you're happy,
and laughter abounds,
When life is a party,
Invite them in.

And they'll go there,
Go there with you.

When you're re sad,
When your heart's a thousand pieces,
When you can't see the way ahead,
Invite them in.

Then wait, see who shows up,
Who'll be there with you.

Mother, May I?

Slow, painstaking
Giant steps like ones
From the childhood game
Mother-may-I.

Or in a pan
Racing downhill
On a snow-glistening slope,
Lightning speed.

Frankly, Lord, I don't
Like either option,
And I want to
Turn back time,

Un-hear the diagnosis!

I can bear it
Only if I can trust you
To be there in the slow, painstaking
Mother-may-I, but especially in the . . .

Racing down the snowy slope lightning speed.

Patient/Tech

She, chatty, trying to
Put on her brave face,
Once again queries the tech
While he's piercing her skin,
Radioactive dye now
Coursing her veins,

"How do you like it,
The new charting system?"
"First day," he says,
"and it's awful—
Ten questions 'stead of one,
Eight minutes, rather than two.
So many problems
All through the system . . .
But what can I say?
We'll figure it out!"

And she wonders,
Will she figure it out?

Inside

"What's it like,
bravely she asked the question,
"someone dying from breast cancer?"

I searched front to back
of my brain, and I recalled
stories, being there in the room.

Not necessarily breast cancer
but I wanted to say
much in common, cancer or any other.

Then I thought of things I'd seen,
sometimes labored breathing,
those looking on thinking each is the last.

Family gathering or no family gathering,
quiet tone in the room
as medical staff come and go.

Encouragement about eating—just a few bites, a sip of water,
the slipping beyond to a comatose state,
those looking on counting the days.

Watching the face for signs of distress
then calling the nurse for another
dose of medicine to ease into rest.

I wanted to say all this,
for I've had some experience, but
I said nothing, nothing at all.

After all, I'm not even sure
that's what she's asking,
not the view from the outside,

Rather from the inside.

I'm Gonna Live!

Fell into defeat
The very moment
I got the
Pink envelope
In the mail.

Why not?
After all thought
I'd heard a
Message straight from
Heaven sayin' won't
Ever have the disease
That killed my mom,
Now here I am,
Biopsy, surgery, treatments.

Recovered, thought
I'd heard
Message straight from
Heaven sayin' "That's it,
No more worries,
Over and done."

Then the phone call
Six years later,
Metastases,
A crushing blow.

Why not
Fall into defeat,
The message straight
From heaven—was it
A lie, or did I
Only hear what
I wanted to hear?

New doctor,
New treatment plan,
A new message,
Is it straight
From heaven?
It says,
You're going to live,
Live long years
Despite the diagnosis!

I choose,
Choose to believe
The message,
After all, the
Messages have carried
Me through the
Rough spots.

Presbyopia

"Presbyopia,"
The doctor says.

I nod
As though I completely understand,
Only to Google the word soon as I can.

Sure enough,
Makes sense
The growing haze.

"Terminal,"
The doctor says.

I nod,
Calmly as though I get it,
But who can get such a thing.

In time
I go about life as though
I can clearly see the way ahead . . .

As though
I never heard the word,
Never heard the doctor say . . .

"Presbyopia!"

Open the Door

I closed the door
To that room,
And I never
Entered there again.

It was too ugly there,
The wires, the machines,
And the smells
So pungent, so horrifying.

Stark terror filled me
As I looked into that face,
Wishing as I stared on helplessly
That the whole scene would change.

I stood there asking myself questions,
"Should I hold her hand?"
"Can I brush away my tears?"
"Am I strong enough for this?"

The pain is too great,
So I invent reasons to leave . . .
Leave her alone as she
Slips slowly away.

I quickly close the door
To that room in my mind,
And I never open it again
'Til I open it with you.

Same ugliness, same pain,
But I can stand it now,
Brush away my tears,
And hold your hand.

A Passing in the Night

Business as usual?
How can it be?
It doesn't seem right,
The whole world should stop.

The whole world should stop
If only for a moment
To take note that
What once was, no longer is.

What once was, no longer is,
But before that point
There was immense struggle,
And I was drawn into the struggle.

I was drawn into the struggle
To save her and I wondered
If the groans spoke of her
Commitment to fight.

In the midst of her struggle
We each secretly
Called to her our support,
But in the end . . .

In the end she died,
In the end, as she slipped away
It wasn't at all what I expected,
Nothing ugly nor gross.

Instead of the ugliness that I expected
There was a peace, a reverence,
A sense of holiness, something that really mattered
Was now gone.

Something that really mattered was now gone
The whole world didn't stop
The rest of the world didn't take notice,
But I was there, and it mattered to me.

Thank you that I could be
A part of your life,
A part of your life,
If only as you pass in the night.

What Does It Take?

What does it take . . .

Detachment?
Determination?
Resignation?
Resolve?

What does it take
To pass from this world
Into the next?

The Young Mother

The young mother,
no doubt, frustrated by political wranglings,
and religious wars within her own denomination,
gave due consideration and then wrote,
"Think I'm going to only post the funny things
my kids say and do!"

Thank God for her, her invitations to escapism,
the antics of her kids giving us room for smiles,
belief that maybe the world isn't so bad after all,
But as we scroll, we see faces of
other young mothers and fathers,
mothers and fathers whose faces are drawn.

They tell their stories
of packing peanut butter and jelly sandwiches,
loading book bags and children into SUV's,
heading off for school drop-off lines
just as they have done hundreds
of other days in their lives.

But for them there will be
no more happy faces to post on Facebook,
no funny stories of their children's antics,
for the day that began with peanut butter sandwich-making
and rushes toward car-riders' lines, and hurried goodbyes
will no longer repeat themselves . . .

Their children gunned down
with assault rifles by a crazed gunman
in hallowed halls of learning.
They plead with us to see not only happy faces,
to hear not only funny stories,
but to be drawn also to their children, now lost—
drawn to stories no one really wants to hear.

They plead with us, beg us on bended knee,
to do our part, to work toward gun control.
to allow children to go to school without fear,
to allow them to grow up,
to have the chance
to have children of their own.

The Wake

Two black-suited men
In a black Cadillac—
They wheel her in,
Place her carefully in front
Of the picture window.

My ten-year-old self
Imagines her to be comfortable there,
That she'll finally get some rest,
After all, I always saw her busy,
Cooking, cleaning, caring for someone's needs.

I wait and the men open the lid,
Fluff and fold and then slip quietly away,
Then I stand beside her,
Tell her to rest,
That she deserves it,
That Granddaddy will be there with her
'Til time to go to the church.

An Unmarked Grave

Perhaps they used
Whatever they had . . .
A stone, some wood,
Your name in white paint
Best they could.

Maybe time, the elements
Were the enemy,
The stone washed away,
The wood toppled,
Paint gone with the rain.

Or maybe it
Was by choice—
Their choice—the ones
You hurt, maybe it
Was their final act
Of shaking fists
Into the air and
Proclaiming that you
Can hurt them no more,
That you are gone
And no marker stands
To say you even existed.

Ultimate Indignity

There I stand,
Kitchen counter,
And the argument begins,
Words coming one side only.

"No, it can't be,
You must be wrong,
I know I didn't forget,
Well, of course, you're right,
I've forgotten many times before,
Despite doctor's chiding
That all must be on time."

So let's think about this
for a moment, went to church
yesterday, so today has to be
Monday! Oh, wait! Did go to church,
But for choir practice,
So that means it's Thursday!

You're right after all,
So I'll push the Thursday
slot and say to you,
"I'm sorry," but to myself
I'll say, "Ah, the ultimate indignity,
Arguing with a pill pack!"

Tsk, Tsk

For some disapproval took the form
Of a simple, "Tsk! Tsk!"
Others saw "Tsk, Tsk!"
To be far too minimal a commentary,
And so they would add,
"A shame really—
Unable to move on,
Stuck in that same place,
Year after year,
Their main point of contact
The support group
They joined the same
Year she died."

Does anyone stop to wonder
If there's something more to offer
Besides critiques or
"Tsk! Tsk?"

Through You

They're not sure
How it happens,
They don't get together
And choose.

But somehow there
Are those special someones
That touch them to the depths of
Their hearts.

Maybe they are young ones,
Ones with much too little time on this earth,
Maybe they're the ones frequently with them, especially
Holiday times.

It's impossible to imagine
The work that they do
Gut-wrenching sorrow always
Invading them.

So today they choose you,
They grieve all of them,
Through you, then they make themselves ready to
Move on.

A Force

They are a force
With which to contend,
A dynamic duo
If you will.

Not in stature,
For slight of size
They are, but
Sheer giants of heart.

Their days filled,
Not with meeting
Patient quotas, rather with
Dedicated time for listening.

And so accolades for you,
Dear Marion, dear Susan,
For ways you care for us,
Body, mind, and soul.

Tribute to Jane

Not just a medical degree,
Not just a specialty,
Rather a specialty
Within a specialty.

Not simply oncology,
Odd as that might sound,
But proficiency in treating
worst of the worst, metastatic disease.

Those degrees that hang
On her wall might be
What got them there
In the first place.

But what kept them
Was how she greeted them,
Offered them
Hope.

Tastes

Do you remember
Those tastes collected
In childhood?
How could you ever forget?

Your grandmother's apple pie
Granny Smiths, butter, and sugar
Melting in your mouth,
How could you ever forget?

Biscuits with ham
And red-eye gravy,
Or perhaps with butter and jam,
How could you forget?

But of late I've tasted
Something altogether different—
The taste of death,
I have survived, but I will never forget.

Take a Casserole

It's what
Keeps us away,
Always a safe distance.

Don't know
What to say,
So avoid them altogether.

After all,
Heard words like,
"Heaven needed an angel."

"Hard now
But soon you'll
Be just like new."

Help me
Find some words,
"None needed," you say?

Show up,
Give a hug,
Maybe take a casserole.

A Sweater with a Hole

She reclaimed
A memory
From childhood,
A favorite sweater.

A sweater with
A tiny hole
Nearly indistinguishable
To all but her.

Unable to resist,
She begins to
Pull a thread
Horrified at the result.

The hole
Grows bigger
And bigger,
And bigger.

"So this . . ."
She says to herself,
"This is my life,
Now."

Shock

It's not the way it's supposed to be,
Not the way it's supposed to be
This time of year.
Oh, we know, we acknowledge
That by now, five days out,
The peace and good will
Are waning a bit.
Toys are strewn on
The living room floor,
And moms and dads are exhausted
From settling sibling battles
While praying that school starts
Sooner than later.

But it's not supposed to be
That five days out there's a
Ten-year-old who won't return
To school—not sooner,
Not later, for she lies
Stricken—he, too—
Gun by his side!

Remember Andrew

Holidays with aunts and uncles—sometimes a bore,
And dreams sometimes escape us—it's factual, it's true,
But remember Andrew,
Sick age four, by eighteen knocking on heaven's door.

Remember storms wiping out our Christmas by the shore?
By contrast remember Andrew,
Every holiday in the hospital with a crisis that was new,
Sick age, four, by eighteen knocking on heaven's door.

Whenever you're stressed, when life seems a chore,
In all the times you're blue,
Remember Andrew,
Sick age four, by eighteen knocking on heaven's door.

The Ravages of Time

Didn't quite know
what to call
this picture of them,

Once tall, some would say stately,
backs straight and
sure-footed steps.

Faces bright, fairly
bursting with smiles,
a joking spirit with all that they'd meet.

But now no denying
their loss in height,
backs bent, steps but a totter.

Eyes now gray,
faces as though a
cloud has passed over.

What shall we call
this picture of them,
the changes we see?

A title that's simple,
a very few words,
"The Ravages of Time."

King Cotton

These days folks worry
Exposure of every kind,
Might be asbestos or smoke,
That dust particles from
The work site may fill
The lungs and gradually
Do the person in.

Not so then,
Times were hard and
If a man had a job
And could take care
Of his family he
Considered himself lucky.

Never you mind the
White puffs that filled
His nose, settled on his clothes,
The silent lung invaders
Produced a perpetual cough,
Brought the dreaded
Diagnosis and a place in
Black Mountain Sanitorium.

The news story
Might have been:
King Cotton
Wins again!

S.I.D.S.

To say special is an
Understatement, first child
And first grandchild, both sides
Of the family,

She'd reached an
Adorable stage where
She cooed as parents
Talked to her.

Incessantly they'd teased
Smiles from her
For their barrage of pictures,
Remember—first child and grandchild.

Believing in keeping to a schedule,
Mom put her down for a nap,
Left music playing
And the door ajar.

Busy straightening the house
She suddenly realized
More time had lapsed
Than her usual nap.

Panic set in the moment
She walked into the room,
No matter what she tried
Nothing could arouse her.

No wonder they call it S.I.D.S.
Sudden Infant Death Syndrome
Is much too
Cruel!

Sylvia and Her Son

Sylvia and her son
Sat stoically on the settee
Centered by the fire
In their living room,
Each tried steering conversation
In safe directions—things like
How good for the sweet
Friends and neighbors
To show up, to bring food,
And to pay their respects,
But the longer they sat
And the longer they worked
At steering conversation in safe directions
The harder it become
To blink back the tears
Stemming from their mutual loss.

My Geranium

She appears so bold,
So steeped in faith,
Whatever the weather
She awakens and lifts
Her bright head upward to heaven.

Sometimes I secretly detest
Those who make life
Seem so easy and faith
As natural as is
Sunrise or sunset.

Then I remember that
For all her current beauty
And seeming life of ease,
She, too, had her moments,
More specifically,
A long harsh winter.

It was an experiment really
When I placed her—pot and all—
In the cold, dark, damp space
Under the kitchen floor and truthfully
Forgot about her.

And I would have
Save for a plumbing emergency
Necessitating a trip

To the dark abode and there I took her
Into my hands, certain of her ultimate demise.

Nevertheless, an experiment is
An experiment, important to see
It through—so there you are—
Your assigned spot in the sun 'til experiment's end and
You're given to the compost bin.

How can it be?
You weathered your winter
And there you stand
In all your glory,
Blossoms lifted heavenward.

Does that mean there is hope
Even for one like me—
One who struggles,
One likely to wag a finger at God for first
One difficulty or another that I face?

Answer my question, dear geranium,
Can I weather my winter?
Can I, like you, lift my head?
Can I bloom
Once again?

Keeping Score

Basketball, baseball, football, and soccer,
From kids on the playground to professionals on T.V.
Someone always does it, serious business you know,
Someone simply, most certainly, must keep score.

This is how it happened for them,
Discovered cancer their oldest son,
Aggressive, so little hope
For a cure.

So they attended him,
Long hospital stays,
One parent always near his bed,
The other home with two younger kids.

Always hoped to make it
Past Christmas, but
Not so for them,
Left his lifeless body and went home to them.

They conjured smiles, then pasted them on,
Wrapped presents, prepared for the morning,
Gave them big hugs, then tucked them into bed,
With them out of sight, they had their cry.

Now surely, most certainly, you'd say,
This is enough, enough for them,
No more bad luck to come their way,
But here's the problem, no one was keeping score.

Not for Sissies

The saying:
Getting old,
It's not for sissies.

Lucky we've had
A lifetime
To ease into it.

There are the aches and pains,
The accumulated losses,
Some through death,
Some through storms,
Some through poor decisions.

Whatever the reason,
The pain of it all
Piles one upon another
Upon another.

And if it weren't for
The courage we've
Mustered along the way,
We'd all have died long ago.

The Master

"Come, come, come!" they all chatter,
"We see the tears, so what is the matter?
Put on some make-up. You're a complete disaster,"
And she vowed she'd do it just like they'd asked her,
But deep within she knew that with words they had bashed her
But without speaking her hurt, she joined in their laughter,
Vowed she'd dig a big hole, cast feelings within, seal them in plaster,
Or send them far away into green pastures,
Who knew, after all said and done, what helps heal hurts faster?
Maybe she'd trust them, maybe in becoming an actor,
In the task of grieving, she'd be the master.

Loved and Lost

Love—
never something to put on a set
of scales, measure gains and losses.

Love
is always taking a risk, throwing
whole self in no matter what lies ahead.

Love
Cherishes every moment, ten years
or ten days with then a tragic end.

Lake Mead

The reporter says it calmly,
Like some casual
Human interest story.

"It's drying up,"
He says, "and what
We're finding are bodies!"

"Questions," he says,
"Emerge for us, like
What happened?"

Accidental drownings?
Murder cover-ups, maybe
Even a suicide or two?

Our thoughts run wild as they examine DNA,
Hopes of news for distraught families who've
Waited too long.

It was only a two-minute news story,
But it brings to mind
Our need to perpetually grieve . . .

Not only lost waters,
But bodies held within.

Life Review

I want to arrange them just right,
Look the best that they've ever looked,
Now, let's see, Sarah's my oldest,
Perhaps she should go first.

I remember when I got her,
Christmases were different then,
Momma made her, stuffed her,
Awaking I found her resting top of my stocking.

Beside her should go Margaret Ann,
Daddy bought her with his bumper cotton crop,
Not really enough money to spare, but he wanted her for me,
I remember his smile as I gave her a hug.

Then goes the bride,
Funny, I never gave her a name,
Guess she was me,
Given me by you on our wedding day.

Then there's Jo-Jo, special among special,
Bought with love for our baby, but look at him,
Un-mangled, untattered as one would expect,
For baby Joey's fingers never . . .

Funny, they've stayed in the trunk so long
Yet here I stand, taking them out, arranging, rearranging,
At age seventy-two, things look different now,
And I love how they help me tell the story . . .

The story of my life, and as I arrange and rearrange
Each one, I arrange and rearrange the story of my life
As well.

How Long?

They say they are on errands of mercy
That they have good purposes in mind
And yet, when all is said and done,
Black brothers lie still, blood spilling on the ground.

They are charged with crimes,
But the jury is stacked
With people who look and think
Exactly as do they.

And in the end
They simply go free,
No consequences to their actions,
They wake up ready to do more of the same.

Meanwhile victims' families
Wake up to yet another
Wave of sadness, head nods with comments,
"Knew it would turn out like this!"

And I have but one simple question,
A question borrowed from the Psalmist,
"How long, O Lord?"
"How long?"

Entitle

When asked
How might
We entitle
Chapters of
Our lives?

Maybe the
Good, the
Bad, and
The ugly . . .

The ugly
Reserved for
The deepest
Of sorrows.

Happy Thoughts

Soon as we got the call, we
Drove the distance to their house
Our friends—older friends and mentors.
Something compelled me to his room
Where the unthinkable had happened.
Curiosity? Confirmation that the unthinkable
Had really taken place? I don't know,
But what I know is that folks were
Insistent that I not enter the room.

People are superstitious,
'Specially about pregnant women,
How they must think happy thoughts,
See happy things—you know—
So the baby comes into this world
A happy baby, so the baby grows
Into a happy person.

So my job that day was to stay the distance
From the bloodied room, the crime scene
Of his own making, but to spare no
Distance from his mom, my friend,
Who would live forever asking herself
Questions, like, "What could they have done
Differently?" and worst of all this one,
"Did I not think happy enough thoughts
When I was carrying him?"

You can bet there was that part of me
That wanted to ask questions as well, like,
How can I these nine months
Soak in only happy thoughts,
See only happy things happening
In the world around me, but, of course,
That thought was not entirely happy
So I brushed it away.

The Doldrums

Along with
the preschoolers
I sang
the song
pitched in a minor key,
and it
did a
remarkable job
of capturing
the doldrums
of a rainy day.

Raining on Sunday,
raining on Monday,
raining again today.

If only,
If only I could
find a song
to capture
the doldrums
of today!

The Light

I look through
The tall trees,
Much higher than
the house.

I am looking
But trying to avoid
Full force of
the light.

I shift my gaze
Not to avoid the light altogether,
But just as it settles on
Outer branches.

There I spot
Subtle colors creeping in,
Brilliant red and a
Gentle gold.

I have spent many seasons
Gazing through the trees and one day
I will let myself be drawn into
The light.

Hurricane Ian

I won't hold back,
I'll call you who you are,
An abusive husband,
You bluster in,
You scream your torrents,
You raise your hand
In threat and enjoy
Our scattering to avoid
Your wrath, and then . . .
Then you retreat and
Show up again,
The good guy . . .
The glistening sea.

What Thoughts

What thoughts flood a person's mind?
It may be minutes, even seconds
When it is clear he or she will
Die but death hasn't yet come.

What did he think about—
The gasoline lantern
Overturning and pressing
Their decision to swim to shore.

No doubt as they began
Their strokes they felt
Adrenaline kick in and
Confidence in well-honed skills.

But as he began to tire,
As he witnessed shore
In what seemed miles away,
What them?

Did he call upon God,
Plead with God
That he needed to get home,
Get home to me?

Did he tell God
It was important
Because I could
Never remember him?

Blessed Sleep

It's a curse,
Lying down, turning,
Fluffing the pillow,
Turning, one side,
Then the other,
Pushing the remote,
T.V. on, then
Changing channels, listening,
Eyes closed then
Eyes opening, searching
For the remote,
Then T.V. off,
Getting up and
Finding a snack,
Back to bed,
Then wee hours
Of the morning,
Finally, finding blessed
Sleep, now wouldn't
It be wonderful
To be young,
Again, able to
Find blessed sleep
The very moment
You lie down.

Chapters

I've written them
Fifty-one chapters and holding.

One for our dating life,
Fifty for years of marriage.

Now I am waiting,
Waiting, waiting, waiting.

It seems I have writer's block,
For who can imagine the next chapter . . .

Without you.

Empty

Too bad
She never had
A kiss,
A hug,
Even a caring word
To give him.

Tried to
Fill the blanks
With things,
Empty gestures,
And heaps of expectations,
Leaving a void.

And so he searches
Day in and day out,
Hope against hope,
For that which he cannot have.

Aimless Chatter

I am alone
In my thoughts,
With my feelings.

No one dares
Go there with me.

Aimlessly, we chatter
About the weather,
Other things, but nothing that really matters.

No one touches
Important parts of my life.

So more and more I cut off
Precious thoughts and feelings,
I become numb.

It's then I chatter with them
All the more.

Comfort and Care

Nights on end
I roam the house
struggling to find
a soft spot
on which to lie,
side effects, after all,
of the life-saving drugs,
are pains that keep
me awake nights on end.

I land on the sofa,
brown, non-descript,
ugly against the bright blue walls.
But who cares?
It's the softest place
on which to land.

Minutes later she's
there with me.
Now understand that I
don't always speak
her language,
but key phrases
I comprehend.

This one happens every night
as I land on the
ugly brown couch,

This particular "meow"
says, "I'm not sure
of my footing,
so move the blanket
so I can jump up."

I oblige, thinking how nice
it is to have the company,
and each time I
marvel that never
before my diagnosis
did she ever snuggle
nearby, and every time
I wonder, "How?
How does she know?"

She makes her way
to the top of the couch.
It's soft there too,
and she's hollowed
out a nest for herself.
She knows that I never
fluff it up nor vacuum
white wisps of fur
from the fabric.

It's her spot,
and I'm glad
she's there,
me the object of her
comfort and care.

Deer in Headlights

He,
The ripe age of eighteen,
Received the clipboard
Shoved roughly into his hands,
His instructions to check off
Names, this motley crew,
As they board the bus,
Fort Jackson the ultimate
Destination.

He,
With his eyes growing wider,
Takes note of rowdiness,
Some of the crew
Finding no way to express
Objection other than
Smashing a window back of the
Bus.

They,
For their acts of protest
Earned themselves
Sets of handcuffs
And MP escorts,
When they arrived at the
Fort.

He?
Well, he—the designated leader—
Won a reprieve from immediate
Poking and prodding,
His military physical,
For, after all,
He was a witness at their
Trial.

He,
Though, soon enough,
Found his way
Back in line,
Dressed in his skivvies,
He followed directions
From army personnel
While all the time
His mind played
Dual reels of
Service in Vietnam
Or the path to
Canada.

He,
So attentive to
The dual reels
Playing out in his head,
Did a double-take
As the doctor
Shouted one last
Instruction.

He,
To this point
Had passed all the tests,
His destiny seemed clear
When the doctor
Noticed something askew.
And so he shouted,
"Wait a minute!
Wait a minute, son!
Walk for me,
From here to yon!
And if you please,
Now raise your
Toes."

He,
The doctor
Could be heard
To exclaim,
"I'll be damned!
Who'd expect
Such a thing—
Unable to raise
Your toes the proper height,
A clear indication of a faulty Achilles
Tendon."

He,
Then, taking his paper
Firmly in hand
Made a quick stroke,
The sweetest message

Any eighteen-year-old
Could hope to receive:
4-F.

He
Could scarcely
Take it in,
And even when
He boarded the bus,
The bus headed home,
Some might say
He still looked
Like a deer in
Headlights.

Afghanistan

Young,
Struggling to graduate,
Certainly, no desire
For college,
He wondered,
"What next?"

Family,
Desiring to guide,
Provided bold suggestions,
"Maybe military
Is right
For you!"

Proudly
He proclaimed his
Patriotism, his joy,
For enlistment
In the
U.S. Army.

Naively
He packed bags,
Headed for training
Proclaiming that
It will
Be fun!

All
Family members rejoice
About completed training,
Wonder where
He'll go,
Next assignment.

Day
Arrived, training finished,
Letter in hand,
His next
Overseas assignment . . .

Afghanistan.

Antennae

Your antennae are always out
Scanning your environment
And searching for those
Different from yourself.
And so you found him
And labeled him,
Branded him
L-I-B-E-R-A-L.

And I feel sorry
For you
Because your antennae
Kept you from getting to know him.

Acts of Will

There are those acts of will
All of us must somehow perform
When someone we love
Dies and leaves us behind.

My mother made cornbread—
Most every day,
Until she died and left
A hole in my dad's heart.

He moped about, while
We watched helplessly,
Worrying 'bout insignificant things,
Who would pay the bills?

Who would clean the house, fix the meals—
All the things my mother had done,
While really we should have worried
'Bout who could possibly fix the hole in Daddy's heart.

But one day we went for a visit.
He cooked a pan of cornbread,
And put it in front of us,
Not just cornbread, but his act of will.

Hard Job

It's one of those
Hard jobs but someone's
Got to do it
Kinds of things.

He watched them go—
Sisters, brothers, neighbors, friends
Marched from this world
Into the next.

Some vowed he was lucky,
Said, "Good genes, hearty stock,"
He never corrected them
But hated his designation, "The Elder."

Broken Relationships

Sick,
She painted on her smiles,
struggled through her hard days,
Doing chores with rest periods
Longer than the chores themselves.

Justice,
You might think would
Afford her warmth and hugs
And care from those,
Her family, yet,
Not so with them.

Broken,
That's how we'd describe them,
And it might surprise you,
But brokenness doesn't fix itself
When sickness comes around,
Instead, brokenness, a disease in and of . . .

Itself.

An Empty Chair

She, their only child,
They, having grown up
in poor homes, they vowed to do
everything right by her.

They read her books
for hours before bed,
and over and over told her
how smart she was.

Talked about how great it would be
to apply for college,
spend four years studying,
a bright future ahead.

She, their only child,
adopted their dreams for her.
She studied hard, and they celebrated
acceptance and a scholarship to the college of her choice.

Graduation approaching, they sent announcements
to everyone they knew,
made reservations for travel,
hauling gifts in their car even months ahead.

Graduation day? They flashed her picture,
on the overhead screen,
Should anyone see the chairs arranged
on the gymnasium floor . . .

They would have seen an empty chair,
save for a hat and a gown draped there.

Best and Worst of Thanksgivings

How can it be—best and worst in the land of the living?
They cooked and they ate the leisurely way,
Time together, the three of them celebrating Thanksgiving.

Noisy breakfast preparation, the cooking and clanging
Making big, fluffy pancakes—just the way to start their day,
How can it be—best and worst in the land of the living.

Dishes in the sink, lunch preparations beginning,
Turkey in the oven, cornbread and biscuits for dressing on the
way,
Time together, the three of them, celebrating Thanksgiving.

The meal now done, Mom washes the dishes while in Dad's mind
new thoughts are spinning,
Grab a coat, hat in hand, to the car they make their way,
How can it be—best and worst in the land of the living?

Foot on brakes, hands ten and two, who knew would be their very
last lesson in driving,
Curious—driving hints, also lessons in life—on both Dad had his
say,
Time together, the three of them, celebrating Thanksgiving.

Round out the day with oyster stew, and dad says best three meals
ever, any of his Thanksgivings,
Says "Goodbye," 'stead of "Goodnight," but son thinks it an easy
slip, things happen that way,
How can it be—best and worst in the land of the living?

Son, awakened suddenly, "What could it be, that heavy thudding?"
Trip to the bathroom, Dad's lifeless body, sight stuck in his mind to this day,
How can it be—best and worst in the land of the living?

Time together, the three of them, celebrating Thanksgiving.

Child of Mine

She was never any more mine
Than when her heart was broken.

That's when we took long walks
And looked at her life
Like a garment
Whose threads are unraveling.
That's when we took other walks
And looked at ways
That weaving might take place
All over again—
First one pattern and then the next.

She was never any more mine
Than when I held her children,
And listened intently
To their silent pain
Supplying appropriate
Things both for hugging
And for smashing as the need would arise.

She was never any more mine
Than when I choked
Back tears for her
And when I called silently
To God on her behalf,
When I fought back
The desire to say—

As I did when she was a child—
"It'll be all better
In the morning!"

Easter Sunday

Easter Sunday—
supposed to be
A happy day,
Go to church
Then home to
A table filled
With dishes she'd
Prepared all week.

She suspected
They'd eat, then
Lie down for
The usual
Sunday afternoon nap.

Instead of sleeping
They'd talk more
Of names,
It seemed to be
A never-ending topic
These days,
After all no name
Seemed just right
For this, their first!

Who knew
Easter could be
As bad as this?

Trip to the bathroom,
There it was—
Blood!

Brutal

"Brutal"
She thought,
"How can they
Say such things!"

Surprised,
They turned away
And wondered,
"Why the tears?"

Consoling?
Hadn't they
Provided consoling words?
Hadn't they tried?

Helpful,
Their telling
Her she could have
Many more children?

Aunt Louise

Granddaddy, he set the bar high,
Lived ninety-five years—seemed like fifty—it's true,
His daughter? Thought she'd make it, make it too,
Maybe break the family record—only three years shy.

Along came Covid, and in her began to stir,
Deep apprehension—concern they'd come home,
And bring the virus with them,
That fight as hard as she might, it soon would overtake her.

But they were careful, wore their masks,
Took off their work clothes and washed their hands,
Exercised precaution, well as folks can,
But one day she fell and broke a bone. Then we were left to ask,

"How can it be—something so unfair?" But we'll go on, her story
we'll share,
Loaded her into the ambulance, a trip to the hospital,
Where she did well and began to heal,
But to gather her strength to rehab she went, and there . . .

There she caught Covid-19, and though it was difficult for them to
see,
They dutifully visited, peering through the window, her bed near,
They called out encouraging words but, truth be told, she rarely
could hear,
Occasionally she smiled but always a struggle, and soon she
begged,
"Dear God set me free."

Covid, dread covid, under our breath we whisper to you,
How we hate, not only how you took her, but also how you made
it entirely unsuitable
To remember our dead, to schedule a funeral.
The funeral—salve for our souls—you stole that, stole that too.

And because of that, we are left,
Holes deep within,
And we hope that eventually we win,
That we find salve for our souls. But now? Now entirely bereft.

A Better Day

When you
feel like it
get up,
embrace the day.

When you
feel like it
say thanks,
celebrate your life.

When you don't
feel like it then
don't dare be
dishonest about your pain.

Scream top of
your lungs and shake
a fist frantically
into the thin air.

Whatever it takes, do it, settle then
into your pillow.
dream, hope, pray, live . . .

For a better day.

Bad Genetics

Bad genetics,
He decided he
Would never go like dad,
Age fifty, clutching his chest.

Planned runs,
He circled the neighborhood,
Soon the entire town,
Then strength training to follow.

Light weights
First, then adding on
The pounds 'til one day
She came home . . .

Called him
But no response,
So she went upstairs, and
There she found him.

Offsetting genetics
Played a trick on him,
Crushed beneath his barbell,
Dead, age thirty-two.

Died Anyway

They rallied behind
him,
the whole family.

A routine physical, doctor told
him,
Doesn't look good.

They used their influence, surgery for
him
in a matter of a week.

Recuperating from surgery they took
him
food—soup, casseroles, treats for all of them.

That was the easy part, then for
him
months and months of chemo.

Then doctors gave
him
more bad news.

The chemo had stopped working for
him,
Proposed stopping treatment and entrance into hospice.

They couldn't stand this assignment for
him,
for her, the three young boys.

So they did their research sought anything to help
him,
Then they sent him off to Mexico for experimental treatment.

All the while he asked for prayers; they gave them to
him,
And when bedridden, the priest brought daily communion to
him.

And here's what I say about
him,
If love could cure, then surely he'd be well;

Yet, he died anyway.

Good Book

I always hate
reaching the last page
of a good book.
for I am lost in all
the chapters as they
unfold and I want
the story to go on
forever and forever.

But we all know
that the last page
is inevitable,
that no matter
how much we
love the story,
no matter how we
fit ourselves neatly
into the life of
the main character
and want her story
to know no end,
on the final page
she is lost
to us, and we
must find ways.
to go on.

Together we have
written a good book,
We are the main characters
with many more beloved ones
along the way, but soon
you must begin
a new book, the two of us
having turned the page
to the last of the volume
we wrote together.

There's the Old Joke

There's the old joke,
The old joke about the pastor
Lying in bed, offering reasons
Why it's a good idea to keep sleeping.

Number one, "It's always cold,"
Number two, "People say mean things behind my back,"
Number three, "I just don't feel like it."
Spouse's response, "Not cold. Some say good things, You're the pastor!"

It's the season of voting,
And pastors worry secretly, sometimes out loud,
"Which way will they go? How will they vote?"
"Will they keep on living and working together? Go their separate ways?"

The secret part?
"Will I keep having a reason to get out of bed on Sunday mornings?"

There's a Sorrow

There's a sorrow so deep, so wide,
Whose weight on my shoulders I cannot hide.

A spouse or a child given over to death,
Witness to the beloved taking the very last breath?

A home caught in a ravaging wind
Trees crashing, unable to bend?

Even a job lost at a critical age,
With very few hopes of turning a new page?

No, it's not one of these, a familiar loss,
Instead, we look up and see the cross.

As we sit where we've sat for decades on pews,
It's time to read, read ourselves the news . . .

We've done our best,
Stood the test.

Now it's time for our church to close.

Ode to the Church That's Closing

Together
You worshiped God,
Made music,
Loved each other,
Welcomed pastors,
Served the needy,
Said prayers,
Made scrumptious meals,
Held weddings,
Grieved the dead.

Closing,
You give thanks
One another,
The good done,
Blessed chapters,
God and you,
When sad,
You look back,
Bow heads,
Say thanks again.

Bump on the Head

You hear stories
'bout people who get
a bump on the head.

They forget themselves,
can't remember their names,
things, then, never the same.

The people nearby,
ones they have loved,
try reminding them their identity.

But it's futile
despite how they try,
No matter how many times . . .

They say, "You. . .
you're a United Methodist,"
they shrug shoulders and go.

Consensus, What's That?

Someone
Made the suggestion, but we
Practically booed them out of the room.

Consensus?
What's that? Why, we've always
Simply taken a vote!

Remember?
Remember how we decided to buy property,
Move together out of the storefront?

Remember?
Remember how all of us decided to take discretionary funds
To help send young guys on a medical mission?

Remember?
Remember how we've always done it,
Not consensus, but taking a vote!

Ignoring,
How we all but booed him out
Of the room, he offered a few simple words . . .

Different
This time, not moving together for good,
But divorcing one another!

Vote

Vote,
Vote, we're here
To take a vote,

It's
Our very best trait, you know,
Discovered it long ago.

Color
Of the nursery carpet,
The paint on sanctuary walls . . .

We,
We certainly can't
Wait 'til it's our turn to vote.

Oh,
So not that kind
Of vote this time?

Not
Something we can
Change with the very next vote?

So
It's something even our children
Will remember even when we're gone?

Remember
That we voted to go separate ways,
Divorce our brothers and sisters of faith.

Charred, Not Consumed

Sacred space,
dedicated to worship,
given to singing,
to prayer.

What then
do we say
when such space
is gone,

When flames
fan such fury?
Silently they asked,
"Now what?

The church,
though, not defined
as a building
but as people,

They, combing
through debris found
the processional cross,
charred, but

Not consumed.

Dark Night

God gave the sun to rule by day,
And the moon to rule by night.

So what's wrong here?
How can it be the moon never shows up?

How can it be we are plunged into darkness
No matter what we do—denial, escapism—nothing works.

Our hearts hurt so badly that
We can't see the way ahead.

Maybe that's why they call it,
Dark night of the soul.

Enough

When do we
Say, "Enough!"

We tell ourselves
We will cope
By indulging only in favorite foods,
Whiling away time with old movies,
Listening to the chatter of others
Though we don't feel like talking.

But still
There are the meds,
Pain in spite of them,
Persistent decline.

When do we
Say, "Enough . . .

Of life!"

Guess I Thought

Shock, absolute shock
About the terminal diagnosis.

Sadness, it sets in,
Tears erupt unbidden.

Attention, focus given to practical matters,
On work to be done.

Searching, reading the literature,
Insistence the doctor must be wrong.

Attention, this time to family,
Wondering how they'll manage.

Care, throwing my arms
Around them every chance that I get.

Wondering, how can this
Be so hard?

Reflecting how through all of life
Taught that we all must face our ends.

Denying, guess I thought
I'd live forever.

Domino Effect

We are the sum
Total of all our days
Lined up in a row
And falling in upon one another
Until finally one day
None remain standing.

For Tomorrow

Most mornings,
Cup of coffee, paper and pen
In hand, I begin to give shape to
My day.

To-do lists,
They are helpful for me and for you,
Help us stay focused on what we
Need do.

Besides that,
Joy in checking things off,
One by one, unfinished tasks rolled over to the
Next day.

What happens,
Lord, when I've finished
My list, nothing to roll over, nothing
For tomorrow?

End of the Line

We've all heard of them,
Those stations referred to as . . .

End of the line.

Young and old alike,
but especially the young ones,
might wish to travel further,
to explore distant places
along the track.

Yet, each in his or her own way
realizes the infeasibility
of such a thing,
for there it is
in plain view . . .

End of the line.

No doubt,
Each, young and old alike,
Must exit.

How will I feel
when I get there?
Frustrated?
Hope against hope to travel further?
Satisfied?

The journey, after all,
having been a meaningful one?
And what will be
my thoughts?
Anticipation of seeing
once again those
who arrived before
me at the . . .

End of the line?

End of Me

Initially,
I worked fast and furiously
On our old house,
Scraping, sanding, painting.

Afraid
That I simply
Would run out of time
Before I got it all done.

Wisely,
I began to slow my pace,
Stretching out for weeks what once
Was done in a day.

Fear
Now runs a different direction,
That when the list runs out,
That will be the end, end of me!

Diagnosis

I'm guessing they've been there,
though I can't say for sure.
Maybe simply a word or a phrase,
maybe a jumble or completely a haze.

Working double-time, a brain,
struggling and feeling insane,
But here they are, set straight and true,
containing meaning for me and for you.

The encouragement they whisper brightly to me,
Say, "Good things come, clear out of the blue,
It may seem like certain disaster,
But you—bet you will prosper."

The diagnosis—it surely is grim,
So I've been reticent to listen to them.
But as if testament to things they have spoken,
The stories, the poems—words, they are flowing.

Somehow—I don't understand it all—
But the words are like an urgent, irresistible call,
In the morning and on through the night,
They arrange themselves on the page just right.

And I am led to believe that now, even when I die,
My stories, my poems will help you see through the lie,
It's true, life not always a full bed of roses,

But please disparage the thought of no good coming through a
bad diagnosis,

For here are my words
That might not otherwise have been written.

Thank You for the Ride

More joy 'bout trains than anyone I know,
Vowed he'd buy a ticket and off he would go.

Sometimes engine straining hard up a hill,
Or zooming down the other side—never got his fill.

Mountains and valleys, points in between,
Folks looked up and waved whenever he was seen.

Passengers would come and passengers would go,
But he never got off, you know.

Year after year, January to December,
Not simply a passenger, rather like a crew member.

People took bets as to when they might see
Him exit the train, same as you, same as me.

One day, graying hair, a tear in his eye,
With a sound, an audible sigh,

They watched as he brushed the tear from his eye,
And made a smile from the audible sigh.

Legend has it his feet stepped off the platform and there he died,
But not before he tipped his hat, said, "Thank you. Thank you for
the ride!"

About the Author

Shirley Biggerstaff Wright is a retired minister who pastored more than twenty-five years in the North Georgia Conference of the United Methodist Church in addition to having had previous experience as a chaplain in both the college and hospital settings. She earned her DMin degree from Erskine Seminary, Due West, SC, her dissertation topic involving the lament Psalms and grief. She earned her MDiv from Candler School of Theology, Emory University, Atlanta, GA. Poetry has long been a hobby of hers, but a metastatic breast cancer diagnosis prompted a deeper commitment to poetry writing, both to assist in processing her own emotions and also to help others struggling with their own issues with grief. She is married to The Reverend Dr. D. Kenneth Wright. They have three adult children, twelve grandchildren, and a cat named Sunshine.

www.ingramcontent.com/pod-product-compliance
Lightning Source LLC
LaVergne TN
LVHW051129080426

835510LV00018B/2322